Slice of Paradise

Collection of Poetry & Quotes.

Written by s.hukr

Slice of Paradise

Publisher: Fajr Noor © 2024

All Rights Reserved

ISBN: 9780645349979

Designed & Authored by s.hukr

Website: fajrnoor.com

Slice of Paradise

Salam.

I hope you find peace, wisdom, and love through these words. I hope this book inspires you to love yourself, educate yourself and become a better Muslim.

May Allah guide you toward that which is best while making your Dunya and your Deen easy for you.

If there is a word that you do not understand, simply search the definition of the word on Google.com.

e.g. "Define [word]"

fajrnoor.com

Slice of Paradise

When you're on good terms with God.
You literally have nothing to worry about.

He will take care of you. You will become reliant on His generosity, His mercy, His safety, His promises.

But most of us get worried and afraid because our connection with God is weak. It isn't the best that it could be.

Our souls know this too well. That's why worries and fears of things other than the divine consume us.

We panic, we get all afraid, we become reliant on others, and we start pointing fingers at everyone except ourselves.

All because our faith isn't as
strong as it should be.

s.hukr

Slice of Paradise

Faith is more than just "I believe in Allah".

Faith is a duty to be the master of ourselves, to become victorious in every aspect of life.

Faith is the reason why we need to strive for success in this world. To be the best that mankind has ever seen.

We need to stop representing our flags and start representing Islam; the best civilisation to walk this Earth.

s.hukr

Slice of Paradise

Life is full of problems. Everyone has them and it's up to you how you address them.

You can sit there, complain, and argue about your problems. Be ungrateful and watch how more problems enter your life.

Or you go and work towards a solution in a healthy manner. And when you do find the solution, do not expect your life to be free of problems.

Another problem will come about.
That is the life of this world.

Your ability to manage and problem solve your life's problems is a skill you **need** to master early on in life.

Otherwise, you will struggle and complain for the rest of your life.

s.hukr

Slice of Paradise

Your character is as important as your Salah.

If your character is bad, you may never see Jannah, no matter how many times you pray.

Let that sink in.

s.hukr

Slice of Paradise

People make time for who they want.
Remember that.

I see this in myself, some people I avoid at all costs and others I would rush to meet.

It's not because I hate people, it's just that some occupy more space in my heart than others. I think the solution is that you become such an attractive soul that you occupy space in everyone's heart.

s.hukr

Slice of Paradise

Pretty privilege is a thing.

The concept that people who are more conventionally attractive have more advantages and are perceived as higher status.

Which is true, if you are well groomed, clean and your appearance is above the social standards, people will inherently treat you better than someone who isn't. Beauty encourages trust.

However, that doesn't mean one should show attitude and think they are better than others.

To use their beauty as an excuse to be unkind and disrespectful. People like that do not deserve your attention and you need to stop giving them it.

s.hukr

Slice of Paradise

I am not impressed by beauty anymore.

It is not difficult or extraordinary. However, if you have the ability to inspire me, to stimulate my mind and make me a better person, well, that makes you a quite admirable.

s.hukr

Slice of Paradise

Help people in silence.

The world doesn't need to know how good you are. Allah knows and that's plenty.

s.hukr

Slice of Paradise

Don't ask a man his salary,
a woman her age, or young
person why they are still single.

We can't control those things,
we can only strive.

s.hukr

Slice of Paradise

How many times do you have to neglect your salah to realise you are closing the doors of Jannah on yourself?

s.hukr

Slice of Paradise

God created women to be beautiful.
Yet this generation of women are
so insecure about their appearance.

O Muslim women, please understand,
that you can be covered in a veil with no
makeup, no adornments, not seeking
validation and still some man will
find you attractive.

And wouldn't you rather a man who values
you for personality and heart? than to
value you for your physical appearance?

You don't need lipstick, lip fillers,
shaped eyebrows, longer lashes, fake nails or
whatever this Dunya tries to sell you.

Instead of working on your appearance, start
working on your personality and heart.

Fight your inner demons.

After 30 years of marriage, when your physical
beauty has faded, I wanna be reminded of why I
married you. I wanna still be in love with you.

s.hukr

Slice of Paradise

Everyone can be pretty or nice but not everyone can see my soul like you did.

s.hukr

Slice of Paradise

A woman's true beauty is not her outward appearance rather it is her kindness, her eman, her honour, her chastity, her struggle to make the lives of others good and comfortable.

She is strong mentally and spiritually to the extent that when you hear about her, people fall in love with what they hear.

s.hukr

Slice of Paradise

We are all fools in love,
except when we love
God first.

s.hukr

Slice of Paradise

Sometimes, all I want is to experience pure love with someone that I know my heart is safe with.

s.hukr

Slice of Paradise

I'm not a writer but I've authored books.
I'm not married but couples seek my advice.
I'm not wealthy but I have inspired millions.
I'm not a photographer but people still ask
about my camera, it's just my phone.

I am whatever God wants me to be and every endeavour will be mastered. I am feared by some and admired by others.

I am quite simply a man of God.

Who are you? What have you done?
What will be your legacy?

s.hukr

Slice of Paradise

Imagine going home and your wife expects you to sleep with her.

Astagfirullah, I'm going to sleep on the couch.

s.hukr

Slice of Paradise

One day you will understand
why Allah made you wait.

s.hukr

Slice of Paradise

You've been in situations where you thought you'd never make it out but somehow you did.

You must have realised by now that after every hardship there is ease.

But sometimes our souls drift away from our true purpose and need a reality check.

Haven't you noticed how close you travel to God when worries consume your heart? But you tend to drift away when you meet life's temporary joys.

God isn't wrong when He says mankind is impatient and mankind is forgetful. I believe once you overcome the internal struggle of your Nafs, your life will become more fruitful.

s.hukr

Slice of Paradise

The more I spend time in this Dunya,
the more I realise that my soul was
made for a different Dunya.

s.hukr

Slice of Paradise

Crazy how you can be happy, healthy and wealthy today but tomorrow your whole world changes.

How peace can turn into chaos in just a few moments, how a sinner can turn into a sheikh, a beggar into a wealthy man.

We humans try to plan our lives trying to reach a certain ideal, however Allah is the best of planners and we should rely upon Him always.

s.hukr

Slice of Paradise

Ask yourself, do people remember
you because they need you or
because they love you?

Is it the mind that remembers
or is it the heart?

s.hukr

Slice of Paradise

It's okay to be friends with people who you disagree with. You do not have to always see eye to eye with everyone you meet.

Difference of opinion is okay
especially on trivial matters.

Just because you disagree on a topic doesn't necessarily mean you destroy a relationship with someone.

s.hukr

Slice of Paradise

Do not allow Shaytan to disunite us
more than we already are.

s.hukr

Slice of Paradise

Do not give foolish people the freedom of speech. Be kind to them and take care of them but do not allow them to create enmity.

Only the wise should have the authority to rule and maintain kingdoms.

s.hukr

Slice of Paradise

The sky is my canvas.

The soul is my ink.

Let us write poetry until our
books are filled with good deeds.

s.hukr

Slice of Paradise

I think most people are good,
but they aren't great. What do I mean?

Good people tend to be kind to one other and maintain a certain level of morality according to what they think is right.

However, great people are on a different level.

They strive towards إحسان (excellence). I notice a lot of Muslims that are good or okay but not great. It's actually hard to find a great Muslim especially amongst the youth.

I feel we compare ourselves with the non-Muslims or those who are lower than us to make ourselves feel better. But that has only lowered our standard.

We need to stop falling for Shaytan's tricks.

Our goal is not to copy the non-Muslims or compare ourselves with people below us in status but rather copy the Prophet and his lifestyle. That should be our goal.

s.hukr

Slice of Paradise

I think Muslim women **need** to
become educated.

To the level where they can home school
children. Educated in many different aspects
of life with Islamic and non-Islamic
perspectives.

Because frankly the education system is
terrible in most countries. I personally find
many children today, have so many questions
that many parents struggle to answer.

So they resort to external influences that
are not particularly the best.

s.hukr

Slice of Paradise

If you don't know how to raise children, don't have children. If you don't know how to treat your spouse, don't get married. It's that simple.

Work upon yourself until you are equipped enough to handle the responsibilities of Life. Because we will all be questioned and accountable on Judgement Day.

s.hukr

Slice of Paradise

Show Allah your dedication towards the Quran & Sunnah and watch how your name becomes famous amongst the 7 heavens.

s.hukr

Slice of Paradise

Everyone is like a magnet. You attract and you repel depending on your characteristics, your mindset and your vibe.

Ask yourself, what kind of people do you attract and what kind of people do you repel?

Do you repel people by pointing out their flaws, making false assumptions? Do you attract people with your toxic mindset or your lovely character?

What kind of people are you surrounded by? What kind of people do you push away? How do you attract/repel people?

You have full control over who you attract and who you repel.

But I think the best among mankind is he who attracts every soul, even those who are not the best. Maybe your company brings out the best in others and you earn all the reward.

s.hukr

Slice of Paradise

Enjoy your own company.
Be your own vibe.
You enter the grave alone.

s.hukr

Slice of Paradise

Most people don't care about
you unless you have:

Money, Status or Beauty.

Take that away and who are you?

s.hukr

Slice of Paradise

Islam is so beautiful that when you actually follow it with 100% effort, you unconsciously influence people with your character, your speech and the way you carry yourself.

Your mindset, your manners, your success and everything else will invite others closer towards the truth, towards Islam.

s.hukr

Slice of Paradise

Silence your ego and listen to your soul.
Obeying your ego leads to slavery.
Feeding your soul leads to freedom.

s.hukr

Slice of Paradise

Everyday clean your heart.

Seek forgiveness from everyone you wronged and learn to forgive yourself. We are all humans bound to make mistakes.

Just keep learning and growing.
Don't make the same mistake again.

And **never** allow the devil to get between you and God's mercy.

s.hukr

Slice of Paradise

Dreams of a world outside my own
reality is where I find comfort.

Because this Dunya has a bad habit of
hurting you as soon as you get comfortable.

I think this is His way of letting us know that
this Dunya isn't our final destination.

s.hukr

Slice of Paradise

While you're overeating, there are people suffering from hunger.

Start fasting fatty. You'll thank me later.

s.hukr

Slice of Paradise

The ability to sit down with another
soul and talk for hours about Islam is
more attractive to me than anything else.

s.hukr

Slice of Paradise

My heart likes the company of those who are conscious of Allah. Not the judgement type or those with a skewed perception of reality, but those who are gentle, kind and soft inside.

Their presence makes you feel happy.
The way they think, the way they behave is pure. They are wise enough to be humble and strong enough to tell the truth.

I meet them once and I already know they are different from the rest. It's like I found a person from Jannah.

s.hukr

Slice of Paradise

While you're listening to music and going to music concerts, there are people who love listening to the Quran and attend Islamic lectures by those who have wisdom.

Are you a fake Muslim? A hypocrite? A delusional soul? An ignorant fool? How arrogant are you?

s.hukr

Slice of Paradise

Women are a blessing as long as they feel they can trust you, find security in you and kindness in the way you speak and in the way you act.

Never lie to a woman. You don't want to be the reason why they don't trust you. Don't hide things especially when they have the right to know.

Don't be harsh or neglect them. That simply doesn't work in the long term. You're meant to uplift them with patience and kindness, it's far more effective.

Why am I saying this? Because many men of today's generation are stupid when it comes to the women in their life. They follow the same backward and toxic mentally that their forefathers used to have. Yuck.

s.hukr

Slice of Paradise

Help people in silence.

The world doesn't need to know how good you are. Allah knows and that's plenty.

s.hukr

Slice of Paradise

If you do me wrong, I won't say anything.
I blame myself for letting you wrong me,
and I'll avoid you in future.

But if you wrong my family and the people I
care about, then you have a storm coming.

If you seek forgiveness, Alhamdulillah.

But if you do not. Then my silence will turn
into thunder, and you better prepare yourself.

For as long as I live, I cannot allow injustice
to happen to those I have authority over.

I am a Warrior of God.
Who the hell are you?

s.hukr

Slice of Paradise

What are you waiting for? You know exactly what to do, so what's stopping you?

Are you afraid of something other than Allah? Where is your trust in Him?

Move on with your life, stop staying in the past, you're just a traveller on your way to Jannah.

So Keep Moving!

s.hukr

Slice of Paradise

Allah opens doors for His believers
that are perceived as impossible.

It's all about taking the leap of faith and
having full confidence in yourself and in Allah.

And if you don't have that, shouldn't you be
working towards that connection?

s.hukr

Slice of Paradise

Be happy for others, love others in their moments of happiness. It might be the reason why God notices you and sends blessings upon you.

s.hukr

Slice of Paradise

Imagine your mother seeing the naked women that you follow on social media, wouldn't you be embarrassed?

If you said, no. You're not a real man of God.

s.hukr

Slice of Paradise

Chasing success will never complete you.
The art is to have success chase you
and never let it catch up to you.

s.hukr

Slice of Paradise

How many times do you have to neglect your 5 daily Salah to realise you are closing the doors of Jannah on yourself?

s.hukr

Slice of Paradise

Be so close to Allah,
that your Duas always come true.

s.hukr

Slice of Paradise

Every human is given the ability of choice.
A choice between two or multiple pathways.
e.g. Right or wrong, Up or down, this or that.

However sometimes people are blind, and they cannot see these pathways. They are preconditioned to believe that their journey is a one way street.

That is why we should always seek guidance from Allah and from righteous people.

Even right now, you have a choice to continue reading or not. You have a choice to save up money to buy my other books or have a delusional expectation that my books should just fall from the sky.

You **always** have a choice in life and the sum of your choices determines your success or failure.

s.hukr

Slice of Paradise

When you see a person is often silent and avoids people. Yet successful in his deen and dunya. Try to stay close to him. Because he has been given wisdom from Allah.

s.hukr

Slice of Paradise

Tell a Brown girl her hair is black, and she'll drag you into the sunlight to prove it's dark brown.

Tell a Turkish girl that you don't like Turkish food and watch how she disowns you.

And stay far away from the Moroccan girls, I heard they are too spicy to handle.

s.hukr

Slice of Paradise

She was moody, more than usual for the past few days. She was busy and probably the stress was getting to her.

So I went to get her some white roses.

When I gave them to her, she smiled like all her worries went away; it renewed her energy.

Sometimes a small act of kindness is exactly what someone needs.

s.hukr

Slice of Paradise

A lot of problems can be solved just by removing some food, some people, and some habits from your life.

s.hukr

Slice of Paradise

Don't look up and feel like you'll never get there. Look down and be grateful for where you are right now.

s.hukr

Slice of Paradise

A wise man once said:

"Give me your advice, but only in private,
and spare me from advice in public.

For being advised in front of people is
humiliating and something I will never
pay attention to."

s.hukr

Slice of Paradise

Men need to take time to
understand women and women
need to take time to understand men.

We are allies of one another. Not enemies.
We are not the same. We have our own
strengths and weaknesses.

We complement one another. We should be
helping each other and not fighting amongst
ourselves.

s.hukr

Slice of Paradise

Lower your expectations of others, do not hold other people to a high level of morality because you will be disappointed. This doesn't mean you think or assume bad about someone.

Instead have high expectations for yourself, because you know what you're capable of and what you are not. Push your limits every day and don't give up on yourself so easily.

One of your main objectives in life is to work on yourself such that your character, your manners, your knowledge and everything else about you, should invite others closer towards goodness, not to push them away entirely.

s.hukr

Slice of Paradise

Over the years people have said a lot of things about me. Some say I'm nice, kind, or sweet while others say I'm arrogant, mean, rude, cringe or even annoying.

Some describe me in the best way and others in the worst ways. But it doesn't bother me because I'm more concerned about what Allah thinks of me.

He knows the deepest parts of me and what is on the surface. And it is He who will judge me. Thus, I make my **focus** Allah and not what people think about me.

It doesn't mean I have total disregard of what people say. It's more that, I do not allow unfiltered opinions of people to ruin my life.

s.hukr

Slice of Paradise

If you have wronged me, I forgive you.
If I have wronged you, forgive me.

And if you don't forgive me,
I will still forgive you.

Because I wanna see
you in Jannah.

s.hukr

Slice of Paradise

Women love love.

They love the idea of falling in love. They love having their emotions fuelled by someone who they adore.

They love a man who can be emotional with them, care for them. Be sweet, kind and compassionate. They love surprises, meaningful conversations and gifts.

Never be unkind to a women even if she is being unreasonable. A woman's dua is like a gift from the heavens.

Collect as many as you can.

s.hukr

Slice of Paradise

Feeling peace is my love language.

Emotional safety and mental ease are such an important thing to me in this stage of my life.

I refuse to stress over worldly things.

s.hukr

Slice of Paradise

Women are emotional beings.

They will say they are going to bed
but end up crying for 2 hours and
then act like nothing happened.

That doesn't make them weak,
it makes them strong.

s.hukr

Slice of Paradise

Confused minds come from a lack of knowledge. A problematic life comes from not applying the knowledge that you learned.

s.hukr

Slice of Paradise

Imagine women in classic black abayas,
covered head to toe. No heels, makeup
or lash extensions, yet still vibrant in
elegance and class.

The fact that she isn't shouting for attention,
is what makes her so attractive. And if she
speaks to you, your heart has no choice
but to surrender and smile at her kindness.

Because it's the beauty within her that shines
brighter than anything you have experienced
before. The noor is so clearly visible.

Smart, Strong, and Bold.

Somebody you wanna keep
by your side till the very end.

s.hukr

Slice of Paradise

O Ramadan come quickly, our hearts are in need of your remembrance.

s.hukr

Slice of Paradise

Many Muslims want to live like
the west and die like the Sahabas.

But how can you pray for heaven
and live a lifestyle leading to hell?

"You will die the way you lived."

s.hukr

Slice of Paradise

Sometimes a woman's reputation
is all she has, it's like glass. If it breaks,
you can't put it back together.

But Islam isn't like that.

No matter how many sins you
accumulate, if you walk towards
Allah, Allah will run towards you.

If you expect mercy from Allah,
you must be merciful to His creation.

s.hukr

Slice of Paradise

Write with ink sourced from the depths of
your heart. Speak poetry as if you are fluent,
until she understands how much you love her.

But never allow a woman to get between you
and Allah. Too often I have seen men become
slaves of women.

s.hukr

Slice of Paradise

The moment our eyes met,
I found myself lost for words.

If words could describe the
impossible, I would use them
to describe you.

Every time I see the beauty around
your soul, I question myself.

"What good deed did I do to deserve you?"

s.hukr

Slice of Paradise

How beautiful to find a heart that loves you without asking you for anything in return.

s.hukr

Slice of Paradise

Take every chance. Drop every fear.
Conquer every flaw. Win every heart.

s.hukr

Slice of Paradise

Build in silence.
Travel in silence.

Win battles in silence.
Because when you win the war.

Your victory will speak louder
than words ever could.

s.hukr

Slice of Paradise

I came into this world with nothing
and I will leave this world with nothing.

Even this body is not mine
nor is my soul my own. I am
just another creation of Allah.

I hope my lord grants me Paradise not
according to my good deeds but
according to his infinite mercy.

s.hukr

Slice of Paradise

Crazy how quickly people of this world will leave you because of one mistake, a difference of opinion or a conflict.

Yet Allah, the king of kings, will never leave you. He is waiting to forgive all your sins, even if they have reached the skies.

It's true what they say, if you have Allah, you don't need anybody else.

s.hukr

Slice of Paradise

Don't be afraid of verbal abuse or criticism.

Only the morally weak feel compelled to defend or explain themselves.

Let the quality of your deeds speak on your behalf. You can't control what others think and so why bother?

s.hukr

Slice of Paradise

If you want to change your fate,
then wake up for Thajjud consistently.
With a hope in your heart that He will.

How can Allah refuse your Dua in the hours
that are most precious to those that sleep?

s.hukr

Slice of Paradise

The moment you become bored of
this world, your heart will start longing
for something out of this world.

s.hukr

Slice of Paradise

Sad...

When I see Muslim women
being used by irresponsible men.

Sad...

When I see Muslim women allow dating
when they should be demanding marriage.

Please don't allow love to blind you.

s.hukr

Slice of Paradise

Be careful who you open up to.

Only a few actually care,
the rest are just curious.

s.hukr

Slice of Paradise

It's very interesting how people can take something without context and put a negative or positive meaning behind it.

It's actually a good way to see how someone thinks and how they view the world.

Do they see goodness in others despite their apparent flaws, or do they see evil despite their apparent good?

s.hukr

Slice of Paradise

There is a story in the Quran about marriage.

About how a man who was homeless, a fugitive, yet strong, respectable and of good character.

Who did a good deed and won the heart of a lady who melted and sought out marriage with this man.

She was clever. She is the wife of Musa A.S.

There is a reason why Allah mentioned this story in His Book. I encourage you to read the story in detail and ponder over why it was mentioned in God's Book.

s.hukr

Slice of Paradise

Men should **never chase** women.
It's so unethical and westernised.

Instead become such a man that
you receive compliments and that's
how you know she is interested.

s.hukr

Slice of Paradise

When I speak about mercy, love and joy.
Everyone seems to love me and praise me.

But when I speak about death, truth and
judgement day, suddenly everyone dislikes me.

Is it my fault that you are closed minded? It is
my fault that your heart is blind? That you
have limited control over your ego and your
emotions?

I wish you understood life in its entirety.

s.hukr

Slice of Paradise

If you want God's mercy, you must have mercy on His people.

s.hukr

Slice of Paradise

It's better to remain silent and to become observant, to watch for signs or behavioural cues.

It's nice not being like everyone else. It's nice accepting yourself for who you are and being grateful what you aren't.

s.hukr

Slice of Paradise

My books and my writing are as much as a reflection of me as they are of you.

You may read them and fall in love with the ideas or perhaps question them and take the middle ground.

Or perhaps you only see what you want to see and fuel your ego with self-righteousness.

s.hukr

Slice of Paradise

Women used to be fierce, admired for their ability and the beauty they possessed within, but today they sell their bodies for coin, attention, social status or fake love.

All of which are temporary, they try to fill a void that keeps wanting more and more and more. And they have the audacity to call themselves real women.

What a strange world we live in?

s.hukr

Slice of Paradise

A sign of a good person is when he dreads at the face of life but is excited by the thought of death.

s.hukr

Slice of Paradise

There is beauty hidden in
everything you are afraid of.

s.hukr

Slice of Paradise

Being in someone's mind is cute but
being in someone's Dua is priceless.

Travel through this world and win
the hearts of everyone you meet.

The more hearts you win, the greater
the gift of blessings bestowed upon you.

s.hukr

Slice of Paradise

To be exceptional you must be
in a constant state of positive
improvement.

s.hukr

Slice of Paradise

If you're under 20, I recommend you study Surat At-Tawba and then live by it.

s.hukr

Slice of Paradise

It still surprises me how a few words on some pages can liberate people and make them feel loved, grateful and guide them.

I never thought in my life,
I would ever write a book but here we are.
Life is full of surprises and I'm glad I did.

I am aware that my books are not perfect.
Forgive me for my shortcomings.
I am human just like you.

My books are a reflection of how imperfect I am as a human. But also a reflection of my intention to leave this world better than how I found it.

s.hukr

Slice of Paradise

Some people are in desperate need of death.
But those same people avoid death.

They avoid truth and reality; they refuse to
accept it. Their hearts are blind.

They are like sick people
who run away from the cure.

s.hukr

Slice of Paradise

Men in black or white thobes with full grown beards. Going to Jummah salah wearing a sweet scent of musk.

Displaying elegance, class, and unity. Looking like real men, not only in physique but also in knowledge, in wealth, in charisma. Soldiers of God that you do not want to mess with.

Men with kindness in their character.
Admired by some and feared by others.
Disciplined with the absolute truth.

That's the man I want as my friend.

s.hukr

Slice of Paradise

If you're a Muslim girl
who is eager for marriage.

I recommend you study
Surah An-Nur and An-Nisa.

s.hukr

Slice of Paradise

Vibing with someone who has the same energy as you is so damn therapeutic.

s.hukr

Slice of Paradise

Men don't cry.
We bleed teardrops.

You don't know our pain &
we don't always have to tell you.

s.hukr

Slice of Paradise

Sorry if I ignore you when I'm tired and hurt.
That's my way of healing instead of being
mad.

s.hukr

Slice of Paradise

I don't know who needs to hear this,
but you consider deleting pictures of yourself
from TikTok, Snapchat, Instagram, or
whatever social media accounts you have.

Because if you die tomorrow, I don't think
you would want to be collecting sins while
you are being lowered into your grave.

If it's not collecting good deeds.
Delete it, right now.

s.hukr

Slice of Paradise

O Men of Islam.
You say you love Islam.
But where is your Beard?
Where is your Sense of Justice?
Where is your Ambition?
Where is your Ghayrah?

O Women of Islam
You say you love Islam.
But where is your Hijab?
Where is your Haya?
Where is your Obedience?
Where is your Intelligence?

You say you love Islam but
Why don't you embrace it?
Why don't you follow it?
Are you afraid of something
other than Allah?

s.hukr

Slice of Paradise

Your success isn't measured by how many degrees/certifications you have or how much money you make or by how beautiful your spouse is or anything else.

It is measured by how happy your soul is and how happy Allah is with you.

s.hukr

Slice of Paradise

Don't follow the majority of people are doing,
be that top 1% of people who aren't like sheep
but instead are the lions and wolves of society.

s.hukr

Slice of Paradise

7 Things you **need** to stop doing:

1. Stop smoking, swearing, or posting selfies for attention or validation or clout.

2. Stop engaging with the non-mahrams for no valid reason.

3. Stop engaging in arguments that have no benefit, that are a waste of time. Better to say you are wrong and move on with your life.

4. Stop delaying your Salah intentionally.

5. Stop listening to Music. Listen to Quran translation or listen to beneficial lectures.

6. Refrain your tongue from gossiping and talking bad about someone even if it is true.

7. Stop exposing your Awrah. Start wearing the hijab if you aren't already. This applies to men too.

Slice of Paradise

If you love food, start fasting Monday's
& Thursday's. If you love sleeping, start
waking up for Thajjud.

If you love money, start giving more
charity. If you love listening to music,
start listening to Quran.

Because your love for Dunya should not
outweigh your love for Allah.

Otherwise, your heart will break into a million
pieces, and you will end up returning back to
Allah out of necessity.

s.hukr

Slice of Paradise

Death is the destroyer of pleasure.

Remind yourself of death everyday
if you want to become successful.

s.hukr

Slice of Paradise

Some people believe foremost in the scripture of mankind. Their lectures, their papers, their institutions of knowledge and their way of life.

But I believe foremost in the scripture of Allah. In His Quran, His Teachings, His Sunnah, and His way of life. Now tell me which one is superior?

I think you already know the answer. Then why do you live your life like the non-Muslims? Why do you think like them?

Are you a hypocrite?

s.hukr

Slice of Paradise

The only reason why corruption exists in our governments is because of a lack of unity and a lack of unity exists because of lack of divine knowledge.

Imagine if everyone was educated upon the absolute truth, there would be no disparity, no difference of opinion.

Even if people lacked willpower, at least they would all be fighting against the common enemy and united knowing the absolute truth.

That's why seeking knowledge is so damn important that Allah made it compulsory for every Muslim.

s.hukr

Slice of Paradise

I just realised that if the entire Muslim Ummah
stopped doing haram, billion-dollar industries
would collapse overnight.

Imagine, if we all united under the Quran,
how strong & powerful we could be.
Nobody would stand a chance.

Maybe, I'm daydreaming.

s.hukr

Slice of Paradise

O women, why do you show off
your beauty and then complain
about the attention you receive?

Stop posting selfies, stop showing off
your outfit, stop doing things to invite
unwanted attention that you end up
complaining about.

s.hukr

Slice of Paradise

I find it funny how some girls call themselves modest, but they are practically naked.

Clothed yet unclothed. You know what I'm talking about, those yoga pants, tight jeans fitted shirts that have become popularised.

It's one of the signs of Qayamat. And let's not forget the boys who wear short shorts and take shirtless pictures.

s.hukr

Slice of Paradise

No one breaks your heart more than
you do by overthinking every little thing.

You need to stop doing that to yourself.

s.hukr

Slice of Paradise

Give your wife a necklace and she'll never take it off. Give her a house and she'll turn it into a home. Give her money and she'll double it.

Provide for her and she'll satisfy you. Treat her like a Queen and she'll always be there for you. That's the blessing of a Muslim Wife.

s.hukr

Slice of Paradise

If Allah said it's Haram,
your opinion doesn't matter.

List of things that are **100% Haram**:

1. Abandoning Salah
2. Neglecting Hijab
3. Listening to Music
4. Drinking Alcohol
5. Smoking Shisha with the boys
6. Wearing Skintight Clothing
7. Gossiping about someone
8. Getting an interest based loan
9. Going to the Club
10. Having a girlfriend / boyfriend

s.hukr

Slice of Paradise

5 times Salah makes you a Muslim and the abandonment of Salah makes you a Kafir.

I don't make the rules. God does.

s.hukr

Slice of Paradise

There is always a cause and effect.

Things do not just happen for no reason. A child is not just born out of thin air. People don't just become rich by merely existing. Injustice doesn't happen because it's meant to happen.

There is always a reason behind something happening. And using your intelligence that Allah has blessed you with, will help you solve many problems in life.

It will help you understand the cause behind every effect and help you optimise for a desired way of life.

s.hukr

Slice of Paradise

If you want to stay depressed
keep living the way you're living.

If you want to stay poor
don't change your mindset.

If you want to be spiritually deprived
don't make any effort to pray Salah,
to wear the Hijab.

You're practically a hypocrite if you
choose to live life without meaningful change.

Because a Muslim is constantly improving
and changing until he reaches a stage
that leads directly to Paradise.

s.hukr

Slice of Paradise

The struggle with writing words on a piece of paper is that people are not always given tone, pitch, and the mood in which it should be spoken.

You can say the same words "I love you" in a very sweet and romantic way but you can also say in a very violent and angry manner that creates fear.

Words themselves have no weight until you add depth, flavour and spice. I can set the mood and create an atmosphere, but I can't read the words for you. You have to do that yourself.

I like those people who automatically assume the positive vibe when reading, or at least take an unbiased approach.

They have trained their minds to view life from a perspective that good souls love and adore.

Are you a good soul?

s.hukr

Slice of Paradise

In my short life, I've noticed that everyone is running after something. Some are running after a university degree, some are running after money, fame or status. Others are running after love, knowledge or justice.

There are so many things to run after in this world and there is nothing wrong in running after these pursuits of life.

However, as Muslims we must run after pursuits in God's way. Not according to our whims or desires or according to social standards.

Our first and foremost priority in life is to worship Allah and this includes our pursuits in life. Because running after Dunya without worshiping Allah first leads to a life without purpose, contentment, and barakat.

s.hukr

Slice of Paradise

The modern world exploits our insecurities.

It is extremely rare to find a human without
them and when we do find someone without
insecurities, we often think they are lying.
Why is this the case?

Why do we spend money & time hiding our inherit
flaws instead of embracing them. Why do we allow
advertising to convince us that we need a certain
product or service to make our life better.

When in fact all we need is to do a little soul
searching and learn to become comfortable
in our own skin.

I guess if more people did that, it wouldn't be
profitable, and many businesses would quickly
die out. They would, wouldn't they?

s.hukr

Slice of Paradise

I never thought that I would
have such a big impact on the world.

I never thought that I would write books and
people from around the world would purchase
them and actually find benefit in them.

Allah makes things happen that we often find
impossible. So just place your trust in Him and
keep working towards Paradise. And always
expect the best from Allah. He will never
disappoint you.

s.hukr

Slice of Paradise

Why do good souls touch each other
but are unable to meet?

Why do good people leave your life or bad
things happen to good people?

Because this isn't Paradise.

s.hukr

Slice of Paradise

Be the reason someone believes in Jannah.
Be the reason someone strives for Jannah.
Be the reason someone's Jannah
isn't complete without you.

s.hukr

Slice of Paradise

No matter how small or big you are.
We all are capable of influencing people.
Sometimes intentionally and other times unintentionally.

I may influence you by writing about a particular topic or acting in a particular way. Whether you take good from it or bad from it is entirely up to you.

But that doesn't mean we become bad role models for others. That doesn't mean we have total disregard for our effect on other people's lives.

We all have a responsibility to follow Islam, to encourage goodness via our own character, to uphold the absolute truth even if it is against our personal interest.

You never know, your good influence on others might be the reason you enter Jannah.

s.hukr

Slice of Paradise

Idk who needs to hear this but stop
wasting so much time on social media.

Go live your life!

s.hukr

Slice of Paradise

No matter how far away someone is,
I never seem to forget a good soul.

Even though I have terrible memory.
My heart always remembers what my
mind seems to forget.

s.hukr

Slice of Paradise

Do you ever finish praying and lie down on your prayer mat because it feels so nice, and you don't want to leave?

s.hukr

Slice of Paradise

I know many of us are not raised with Islamic teachings, but instead with cultural norms that clearly go outside the boundaries of Islam.

Such people need to stay close to the Quran, rely on Allah alone. Understand God's book because through knowledge and blessings of the Quran you will find a way out.

s.hukr

Slice of Paradise

Salah is the cure for every lost soul that yearns for peace and power.

s.hukr

Slice of Paradise

I think the most attractive feature in a woman is the Haya in her eyes, because hidden in the depths of her eyes is the beauty of her soul.

s.hukr

Slice of Paradise

My sister asked me why do girls get nose rings? I thought about it and gave her the answer she needed.

I told her that they have trouble breathing and that's why need the extra hole. Alhamdulilah she never got a nose ring.

I don't want her to rely on external beauty when her heart and mind should be the most beautiful things about her.

s.hukr

Slice of Paradise

Life is full of tests, trials, and tribulations.

The closer you get to Allah, the
more difficult they will become.

But the more rewarding they
will get every time you pass them.

s.hukr

Slice of Paradise

Making dua isn't going to solve all your problems. You must do something uncomfortable.

You must work towards a solution. All great people throughout history had a very difficult life, but they are still remembered to this day.

Why? Because they didn't just make dua, they actually worked towards whatever Allah guided them towards. They were not lazy.

You need to figure it out by yourself on what the best course of action is.

And if you happen to fail, that's a good thing. Learn from the failure, use it to propel yourself towards your goals.

s.hukr

Slice of Paradise

Every time you give up something for the sake of Allah.

Allah will enrich you from places you never knew existed.

s.hukr

Slice of Paradise

Most issues stem from your family. They are the first contact you have with people in this Dunya.

The way they live their life will in no doubt have a direct effect on your life. Regardless of how good or bad they are.

If they incline to their whims & desires or if they walk the path of righteousness, you will be influenced.

Even if you think you are not like them, sub consciously you have picked up some of their programming and often, others can see the resemblance.

This is why I firmly believe young people need to go out exploring by themselves, especially young boys. Get comfortable being alone.

Far away from all influences and distractions of this world. So we can find our true selves and not become carbon copies of our family.

s.hukr

Slice of Paradise

When beauty begins from the heart,
the deaf will hear and the blind will see.

s.hukr

Slice of Paradise

May Allah bless those people that
chase nobody, need no validation
and mind their own business.

Say Ameen.

s.hukr

Slice of Paradise

Lately, I've found this world so cold,
that whenever I touch it, I crave the
warmth of Jannah even more.

s.hukr

Slice of Paradise

The key to happiness is to always
be thankful for whatever you have.

Always thank Allah.
Always praise Allah.
Always talk to Allah.

The one who created you
understands you best.

Do not worry. Allah will grant you
all of your prayers at the best time.

He knows what is best for you, which places
are best for you and which people are best
for you and knows the best time for these
blessings to come into your life.

The key to happiness is gratitude
and contentment with Allah's decrees.

s.hukr

Slice of Paradise

Eman...

Something so sweet and fulfilling.
Something only the foolish would let go of.
It is complete hope, sincerity, and faith with
the one who is worthy of all worship.

The stronger your Eman, the better life
becomes. You can't see it nor touch it, but
you can surely feel it surround your soul as it
brightens your face with Noor upon Noor.

s.hukr

Slice of Paradise

A real man offers marriage, not flowers,
A real women takes respect, not money.

s.hukr

Slice of Paradise

Imagine a mountain of gold, a valley flowing with wine, milk and honey, a land full of the most stunning people you have ever seen.

Imagine having a life with everything you desire and more. Imagine the life of Paradise.

Such a place will never exist in this world. So constantly remind yourself of life's true purpose.

Why are you breathing?
Why do you get up every day?

Quite simply. Paradise.

It is only promised to us when we live for the sake of Allah. When we do our absolute best to attain the glory of being a True Muslim.

s.hukr

Slice of Paradise

I've realised people who have genuine love
for Deen have a natural glow on their faces.
The Noor is so clearly visible.

s.hukr

Slice of Paradise

Stop using the term "Don't judge me"
to escape religious advice.

It's pathetic. But also stop giving advice
in public when it should be in private.

s.hukr

Slice of Paradise

Preserve your soul.

Be lowkey. Stay private.

Set boundaries. Talk to Allah.

Forgive others. Repent.

Guard your soft heart.

s.hukr

Slice of Paradise

I think it is extremely important for men to understand four things without which their success is not guaranteed.

Understand their duty and obligation to Allah.

Understand the financial system and not become a slave of the dollar or anybody.

Understand women and how to take care of them according to the Quran & Sunnah.

Lastly, understand that they need to constantly strive towards the art of perfection because men are the inherit leaders and role models of society.

s.hukr

Slice of Paradise

You never know, one good deed could be the reason why thousands of people make Dua for you.

Never stop doing good.

s.hukr

Slice of Paradise

You could die tomorrow.
Tell someone you love them today.

s.hukr

Slice of Paradise

I love you.

You're probably thinking:
"You don't even know me."

But if people can hate for no reason.

Why can't I love?

s.hukr

Slice of Paradise

You need to stop overthinking and complicating things that are outside your control.

Enjoy your life. Stop stressing and worrying over temporary things.

Enjoy your life by living your best life, where you grow as a person, practice faith and strive towards success in God's way.

Along the way, enjoy the blessings Allah sends your way and always be grateful.

s.hukr

Slice of Paradise

Tuzlu kahve sever misin?

Çünkü senin o tatlı ellerinden
içmeyi çok isterdim.

s.hukr

Slice of Paradise

I do not consider myself to be special
but people keep telling me otherwise.

Perhaps this is another blessing from God.

But let me remain humble.
I do not want to fuel my
ego with pride.

s.hukr

Slice of Paradise

There are two types of women, one is insecure, and the other isn't. The insecure one allows her insecurities to overcome her principles.

For example:

A woman who dresses immodesty seeking validation through attention. Or causes "drama" because she has to be the winner, the one who is always right. Pathetic.

The secure woman doesn't shout for attention, she makes life pleasant by defusing problems. She is a damn Queen, and she does not need to prove it to anyone. Her dress code, her manners and her speech dictate her high value and status.

s.hukr

Slice of Paradise

Practicing Islam is 100% easy when you're surrounded by righteous people who follow the sunnah.

If you're finding it hard to stay on Deen, have a look at your family and friends.

s.hukr

Slice of Paradise

A person who forgives others easily is a person who knows peace of mind and goes to bed with a calm heart.

s.hukr

Slice of Paradise

Everyday ask yourself, are you
intentionally working towards Jannah?

Is your occupation helping?
How about your family and friends?
Do you need to cut people out of your life?
Do you need to change something drastically?

Is your life structured in a way that you are
guaranteed Paradise, or do you get distracted
by this Dunya and forget your true purpose?

Keep asking yourself until you become
content with dying tomorrow.

s.hukr

Slice of Paradise

There will be people on Judgement Day that will laugh while everyone is worried. They will be sinners like you and me. But the only reason they will be laughing is because they repented sincerely.

Allah has the ability to turn our sins into good deeds. He is more merciful than He is fair. The odds of Jannah are in our favour, how can we lose?

s.hukr

Slice of Paradise

More people need to understand that whoever Allah guides, nobody can lead him astray and whoever Allah leads astray, nobody can guide.

There will be some people that no matter how much you help them, there will still refuse to be guided upon Islam.

And others, no matter how much they are led astray, if Allah wants to guide someone towards truth, nobody can lead them astray.

Ultimately, it doesn't matter what you do or what I do. It doesn't matter if the whole world is good or bad. If Allah wants to lead someone astray or guide someone towards truth. Who are we to oppose Allah?

We just have to do our part, our duty as believers.

Making sure that we guide others by following the example of the Prophet ﷺ. So, we can stand on Judgement Day and say that we did our part.

s.hukr

Slice of Paradise

Be authentic. Be Real.

Notice how I didn't say to be perfect.

People value authenticity, they value those who stay true to themselves even if the world hates them or doesn't agree with them.

People respect those who are firm on their religion. It demands integrity and honour.

Stop caring about what others think about you. Stop trying to please everyone. Your job isn't to satisfy anyone except God.

s.hukr

Slice of Paradise

Do not be afraid of making mistakes, be afraid of what you do after you make a mistake.

Mistakes are bound to happen; we are all human. It's how you handle your mistakes that really matters.

s.hukr

Slice of Paradise

Forgive in a fashion that does not go
unnoticed by the master of mercy.

Forgive as if you have forgotten the crime.

s.hukr

Slice of Paradise

I'd like to think that real Muslim men take care of their appearances. The way they dress, the way they keep themselves clean and tidy.

Cleanliness is half of our faith, and we should be proud to wear clothing that represents our faith.

Wearing a bit of musk and being presentable should be bare minimum especially when you meet others. It's one of the things that defines a man's character. Also, the ladies love a man who is well dressed. It's a win-win situation.

s.hukr

Slice of Paradise

As a man, you have women under your authority/responsibility whom you are legally obliged to take care of.

That means, you are obliged by God, to take care of them in every respect. This could be financially, spiritually, mentally, emotionally and physically.

Due to the responsibility, you have over them, this also gives you a degree of authority over them.

Righteous women understand this.

With that authority, it is your responsibility to ensure that your women are dressed appropriately, obedient to God and educated enough to raise the next generation in the best manner, among other things. As a man you can't abuse that power.

Otherwise, you're in big trouble and your women will not listen to you, cause you headaches and you will wonder why they label you as toxic.

s.hukr

Slice of Paradise

God created women to be beautiful. Yet this generation of women are so insecure about their appearance.

O Muslim women, please understand, that you can be covered in a veil with no makeup, no adornments shown, not seeking validation or attention. And still some man will find you attractive.

And wouldn't you rather a man who values you for personality and heart? than to value you for your physical appearance?

You don't need lipstick, lip fillers, shaped eyebrows, long lashes, fake nails or whatever this Dunya tries to sell you.

They are just poking at your insecurities to make money. Trust me, you are gorgeous, stunning and pretty just the way you are. So much that God made hijab compulsory for you.

s.hukr

Slice of Paradise

I want to remain unknown and strange in the eyes of people.

s.hukr

Slice of Paradise

Allah can take you to the sky and
still bury you below the ground.

s.hukr

Slice of Paradise

For me it's never the place,
it's always the people in the place.

Some people will make a beautiful place dull,
and others will make a dull place extremely
beautiful.

Trust me, it's always the people
the place is always temporary.

s.hukr

Slice of Paradise

Be good to people because they can be your ticket to Paradise.

You don't know how loved someone is by Allah.

s.hukr

Slice of Paradise

A person becomes 10 times more attractive not by their looks but by their acts of kindness, love, respect, and honesty.

s.hukr

Slice of Paradise

Everyone is always doing something.

Everything is so damn quick these days.
People are always busy.

Are we in a rush to collect good deeds
or are we in a rush to do as we are told?

Are we in a rush to enter our graves or
have we been avoiding that topic?

Do we live for short term gratification or
are we living for long term success?

s.hukr

Slice of Paradise

The arrival of Dajjal is actually
much closer than we think.

Have you prepared yourself
for the arrival of Dajjal?

Because you should.

s.hukr

Slice of Paradise

Muslim Guys joke about 4 wives but let's be honest, in reality they struggle with 1 wife.

s.hukr

Slice of Paradise

If you lost someone, go find them.
If you broke their heart, go ask for
forgiveness. If you're broken, forgive
others. Because this life is very short.

s.hukr

Slice of Paradise

Ramadan is not a temporary
increase of religious practice,
it is a glimpse of what you are
capable of doing every single day.

s.hukr

Slice of Paradise

When you're a good person you
don't lose people. People lose you.

s.hukr

Slice of Paradise

Alhamdulillah for the flaws that keep me humble and the sins that keep me repenting.

s.hukr

Slice of Paradise

The best sinners are those
that repent sincerely.

s.hukr

Slice of Paradise

You don't need to be a scholar
to understand Quran.

Allah designed the Quran
to be read by everyone.

If you don't understand Arabic,
start by reading the English
translation.

But start somewhere.

s.hukr

P.S I recommend the Qurans from fajrnoor.com

Slice of Paradise

One of the keys to Paradise is through understanding and applying Quran in your life.

If you haven't already, make a firm commitment into reading 5 pages a day of the Quran with understanding.

You can do this by yourself. Don't worry if you don't understand everything.

In 6 months time, you will easily finish and have a better understanding of how you should be living your life.

s.hukr

Slice of Paradise

Appreciate everything.
Be grateful for everything.

That includes everything
that you don't have.

s.hukr

Slice of Paradise

If you believe someone has a sinister agenda.
Withdraw from them. Disengage from them.
Unfollow them. Block them. Distance yourself
from them.

Stop giving them more attention by telling
everyone how bad they are. That creates more
publicity. Even bad publicity can be good
publicity because people are inherently
curious creatures. This is why gossip is
forbidden.

Don't be stupid. Approach the
matter in a very civilised fashion.

That means completely ignoring them and
distancing them from your life.

s.hukr

Slice of Paradise

The way I care for people makes me wish
I had someone like that in my life who would
drown me in their affection.

s.hukr

Slice of Paradise

If you want to be wealthy
start giving more charity
and being more generous.

God will double your investment.

s.hukr

Slice of Paradise

If you're a man of your word,
you need to watch your tongue.

Your language has consequences
but your words have unlimited power.

s.hukr

Slice of Paradise

Be patient, stop trying to do everything.
Prioritise your life.

Do what you are instructed to do by
Allah first and then follow your heart.

s.hukr

Slice of Paradise

Ask yourself, how many of your friends
remind you to pray your Salah on time?

Well that's how many you need to keep
and the rest you need to cut.

s.hukr

Slice of Paradise

Death isn't when you stop breathing,
rather it is when you are forgotten by
every living person.

Make it a habit to remember
those who have passed away,
mention their names in your Duas.

So when you pass away,
there is someone making
Dua for you.

s.hukr

Slice of Paradise

Be a soldier when you face adversity. Listen to reason and do not be insensitive. Never allow people to bend you to their command.

You are a soldier of God. A servant of God.

If your connection with God isn't making you win in life, then that connection isn't very strong, and you need to do something about it.

s.hukr

Slice of Paradise

Women are not men and men are not women.

Men should not be in their houses taking care
of children while women get the bread.

Yes, men should help and
spend quality time at home.

Equally, women should not be
outside their houses causing
fitnah and wasting their time.

When they should be taking care
of important business inside the house.

s.hukr

Slice of Paradise

Growing up, I had nothing.

I didn't have what most people seemed to have. I didn't have an obscene amount of wealth, fame, knowledge, or anything worth telling people about. I was just grateful for the little things in life.

While life was tough for most of my early years, one thing I did firmly believe in was Allah.

Even though I was lost most of the time, Allah always guided me. Despite my flaws, my sins and the darkness of my Nafs. My lord has always been kind to me and has always guided me through every difficulty.

I think the key is sincerity and continuous struggle no matter what. Today, I write to you letting you know that Allah will never disappoint a Believer. He will never disappoint those who speak the utmost truth, uphold justice and carry out Islam in the best manner. No matter how many people might be against you.

Everything I didn't have growing up, Allah gave me all that and more. That is the generosity of my lord. Strive for His sake and you will not be disappointed. That is His promise, not mine.

s.hukr

Slice of Paradise

It is so difficult to find good people that you find comfort in. People who love you for the sake of Allah and encourage you towards faith.

If have someone like that, you are very lucky.

s.hukr

Slice of Paradise

I want to take you to Jannah with me, because Jannah would be incomplete without you.

s.hukr

Slice of Paradise

Book Recommendations for Muslim Men:

1. The Quran with Translation

2. The Ideal Muslim
   by Muhammad Al-Hashimi

3. 44 Ways of Manhood
   by Taymullah Abdur-Rahman

4. The Productive Muslim
   by Mohammed Faris

5. The Islamic Creed Series
   by Dr. Umar S. al-Ashqar

fajrnoor.com

Slice of Paradise

Book Recommendations for Muslim Women:

1. The Quran with Translation

2. The Ideal Muslimah
   by Muhammad Al-Hashimi

3. You can be the Happiest Woman
   by Aid al-Qarni

4. Women around the Messenger
   By Muhammad Ali Qutb

5. The Islamic Creed Series
   by Dr. Umar S. al-Ashqar

fajrnoor.com

Slice of Paradise

Thank you for reading this book.

I hope that you enjoyed it and found some benefit from my words.

May Allah always have mercy on you and guide you towards the straight path. **Ameen.**

Sincerely,
s.hukr

P.S If you liked this book, you should checkout my other books.

fajrnoor.com

Slice of Paradise

A Sincere Letter to my Admirers

السلام عليكم

to whoever you are and wherever you live.

Without your love, I would not be writing this book and to be honest with you, I was not planning to write again. But I guess, the love you guys have shown me told me otherwise.

I wanted to take this opportunity to thank each and everyone for the support and love you have shown me. Whether it be through purchasing my books, sending me a heart-warming message, leaving a positive review that ends making me smile or even supporting me on Instagram.

I am forever in debt to your kindness. I would not be where I am in life without your support, so I thank you from the depths of my heart. May Allah bless you in ways you cannot imagine, and I pray that we meet in Paradise.

I also have a small favour to ask that I think will benefit you as much as it will benefit me. If my books have inspired you towards a single good deed, then I ask that you spread my books to others and encourage them to purchase it as an investment to their hereafter.

Slice of Paradise

For every time someone gets my books and does a good deed inspired by what I wrote, because of it, you will earn a good deed, and I will earn a good deed.

And every time someone purchases my books, a portion of profits are donated as charity. Collecting even more good deeds, it's called Sadaqah Jariyah.

Sadaqah Jariyah is charity that continues to benefit people long-term and continues to earn the benefactor rewards even after death.

Isn't Islam so beautiful?

إن شاء الله
I hope that with your help, my books spread everywhere and become a source of blessings for me, you and this ummah. I wanna take you all to Jannah with me.

I hope that isn't too much to ask.

Again Sincerely,
s.hukr

S.hukr Books

1. Fajr and Noor

2. Through His Eyes

3. Noor upon Noor

4. Slice of Paradise

5. Mumin Mindset

6. How to Marry a Muslim Girl

7. Divine Love

www.ingramcontent.com/pod-product-compliance
Lightning Source LLC
Chambersburg PA
CBHW030255010526
44107CB00053B/1722